TI

rder.
ed.

Practice question:

1 x 2 = ⬚ 2

The Five Minute Test!

1. 2 x 2 = ⬚

2. 3 x 2 = ⬚

3. 4 x 2 = ⬚

4. 5 x 2 = ⬚

5. 6 x 2 = ⬚

6. 7 x 2 = ⬚

7. 8 x 2 = ⬚

8. 9 x 2 = ⬚

9. 10 x 2 = ⬚

Did you beat the clock?

Check your answers!

1. 4 2. 6 3. 8 4. 10 5. 12 6. 14 7. 16 8. 18 9. 20

When can you buy two yachts for just 10 dollars?
When they're having a sail!

PAIRING UP

Can you complete these problems
using the two times table?

Practice question:

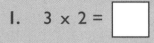

$8 \times 2 =$ | 16 |

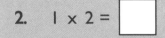

The Five Minute Test!

1. $3 \times 2 =$ ☐

2. $1 \times 2 =$ ☐

3. $2 \times 2 =$ ☐

4. $6 \times 2 =$ ☐

5. $7 \times 2 =$ ☐

6. $5 \times 2 =$ ☐

7. $8 \times 2 =$ ☐

8. $4 \times 2 =$ ☐

Did you beat the clock?

Check your answers!

1. 6 2. 2 3. 4 4. 12 5. 14 6. 10 7. 16 8. 8

What tools do you need in math class?
Multi-pliers!

THREE'S A CROWD

Can you complete the three times table?

Practice question:

$3 \times 3 = \boxed{9}$

The Five Minute Test!

1. $1 \times 3 = \boxed{}$

2. $2 \times 3 = \boxed{}$

3. $3 \times 3 = \boxed{}$

4. $4 \times 3 = \boxed{}$

5. $5 \times 3 = \boxed{}$

6. $6 \times 3 = \boxed{}$

7. $7 \times 3 = \boxed{}$

8. $8 \times 3 = \boxed{}$

9. $9 \times 3 = \boxed{}$

10. $10 \times 3 = \boxed{}$

Did you beat the clock?

Check your answers!

1. 3 2. 6 3. 9 4. 12 5. 15 6. 18 7. 21 8. 24 9. 27 10. 30

What do you call a fish with no eye?
Fsh!

TWOS AND THREES

All these problems use the two and three times tables.

Practice question:

$3 \times 2 = \boxed{6}$

The Five Minute Test!

1. $2 \times 3 = \boxed{}$

2. $5 \times 2 = \boxed{}$

3. $4 \times 3 = \boxed{}$

4. $1 \times 3 = \boxed{}$

5. $1 \times 2 = \boxed{}$

6. $3 \times 3 = \boxed{}$

7. $5 \times 3 = \boxed{}$

8. $7 \times 2 = \boxed{}$

9. $8 \times 3 = \boxed{}$

10. $6 \times 3 = \boxed{}$

Did you beat the clock?

Check your answers!

1. 6 2. 10 3. 12 4. 3 5. 2 6. 9 7. 15 8. 14 9. 24 10. 18

What do you call a sheep with no legs?
A cloud!

TOUGH TWOS AND THREES

More two and three times table practice.

Practice question:

$$10 \times 2 = \boxed{20}$$

The Five Minute Test!

1. $9 \times 2 = \boxed{}$

2. $10 \times 2 = \boxed{}$

3. $11 \times 2 = \boxed{}$

4. $12 \times 2 = \boxed{}$

5. $9 \times 3 = \boxed{}$

6. $10 \times 3 = \boxed{}$

7. $11 \times 3 = \boxed{}$

8. $12 \times 3 = \boxed{}$

Did you beat the clock?

Check your answers!

1. 18   2. 20   3. 22   4. 24   5. 27   6. 30   7. 33   8. 36

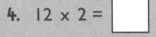

Which one is faster, hot or cold?
Hot, because you can catch a cold!

MULTIPLYING MASTERY

How many feet are there altogether
in the following groups of people?

Practice question:

Three skateboarders? _6_

The Five Minute Test!

1. A pair of brothers? ____

2. A five-a-side soccer team? ____

3. Ten hockey players? ____

4. A seven-person volleyball team? ____

5. Eight athletes running? ____

6. Two six-a-side teams playing volleyball? ____

7. Nine people in a rowboat? ____

8. Six basketball players practicing? ____

9. A team of 11 football players? ____

10. Twelve rugby players? ____

Did you beat the clock?

Check your answers!

1. 4　2. 10　3. 20　4. 14　5. 16　6. 24　7. 18　8. 12　9. 22　10. 24

FOUR'S THE SCORE

Can you complete the four times
table in less than five minutes?

Practice question:

$10 \times 4 = \boxed{40}$

The Five Minute Test!

1. $1 \times 4 =$ ☐

2. $2 \times 4 =$ ☐

3. $3 \times 4 =$ ☐

4. $4 \times 4 =$ ☐

5. $5 \times 4 =$ ☐

6. $6 \times 4 =$ ☐

7. $7 \times 4 =$ ☐

8. $8 \times 4 =$ ☐

9. $9 \times 4 =$ ☐

10. $10 \times 4 =$ ☐

Did you beat the clock?

Check your answers!

1. 4 2. 8 3. 12 4. 16 5. 20 6. 24 7. 28 8. 32 9. 36 10. 40

What's a quick way to double your money?
Fold it!

FAST FOUR WHEELS

How many wheels would you see in each event?

Practice question:

Five old cars racing = `20`

The Five Minute Test!

1. Four sports cars on display = ☐

2. Three Minis racing = ☐

3. A dragster race between two cars = ☐

4. Six old cars in a demolition derby = ☐

5. Ten rally cars flying across a muddy track = ☐

6. Seven stock cars going around a track = ☐

7. Eight antique cars crawling along = ☐

8. Twelve grand prix cars = ☐

Did you beat the clock?

Check your answers!

Why did the car yawn?
Because its wheels were tired!

FOUR TO ONE

This test uses problems from the one, two, three, and four times tables.

Practice question:

$3 \times 4 = \boxed{12}$

The Five Minute Test!

1. $5 \times 3 = \boxed{}$

2. $4 \times 2 = \boxed{}$

3. $7 \times 3 = \boxed{}$

4. $2 \times 4 = \boxed{}$

5. $5 \times 1 = \boxed{}$

6. $6 \times 4 = \boxed{}$

7. $8 \times 2 = \boxed{}$

8. $9 \times 3 = \boxed{}$

9. $10 \times 1 = \boxed{}$

10. $5 \times 4 = \boxed{}$

Did you beat the clock?

Check your answers!

1. 15 2. 8 3. 21 4. 8 5. 5 6. 24 7. 16 8. 27 9. 10 10. 20

Which sort of table has no legs?
A times table!

MISS STAKE'S PROBLEMS

Miss Stake is very forgetful.
Can you fill in the missing numbers?

Practice question:

2 x [3] = 6

The Five Minute Test!

1. 1 x [ ] = 3

2. 2 x [ ] = 4

3. 3 x [ ] = 9

4. 6 x [ ] = 6

5. 3 x [ ] = 12

6. 5 x [ ] = 15

7. 8 x [ ] = 16

8. 5 x [ ] = 20

Did you beat the clock?

Check your answers!

What has two hands but can't carry anything?
A clock!

TIMES TABLE WITH A TWIST

Do the five times table in reverse.

Practice question:

$12 \times 5 =$ 60

The Five Minute Test!

1. $11 \times 5 =$

2. $10 \times 5 =$

3. $9 \times 5 =$

4. $8 \times 5 =$

5. $7 \times 5 =$

6. $6 \times 5 =$

7. $5 \times 5 =$

8. $4 \times 5 =$

9. $3 \times 5 =$

10. $2 \times 5 =$

Did you beat the clock?

Check your answers!

What did the police say about the stolen mirror?
They say they are looking into it!

BUNCHES OF FIVE

A witch has gathered things in bunches of five. How many items does she have?

Practice question:

2 x 5 bears' teeth = $\boxed{10}$

The Five Minute Test!

1. 1 x 5 spiders = ☐

2. 5 x 5 green frogs = ☐

3. 3 x 5 rabbit tails = ☐

4. 4 x 5 moldy cabbages = ☐

5. 6 x 5 newts' eggs = ☐

6. 9 x 5 slugs = ☐

7. 7 x 5 red berries = ☐

8. 10 x 5 blackberry leaves = ☐

Did you beat the clock?

Check your answers!

1. 5 2. 25 3. 15 4. 20 5. 30 6. 45 7. 35 8. 50

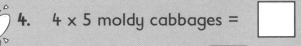

How do really small people call each other?
On microphones!

COUNTDOWN TO BLASTOFF!

Write the answers to the problems in the first column. Rearrange them in the second column, to make a rocket countdown from 10 to 1.

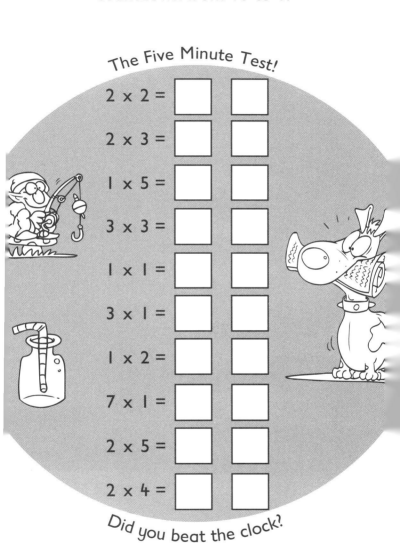

The Five Minute Test!

2 x 2 = ☐ ☐

2 x 3 = ☐ ☐

1 x 5 = ☐ ☐

3 x 3 = ☐ ☐

1 x 1 = ☐ ☐

3 x 1 = ☐ ☐

1 x 2 = ☐ ☐

7 x 1 = ☐ ☐

2 x 5 = ☐ ☐

2 x 4 = ☐ ☐

Did you beat the clock?

Check your answers!

How did the carpenter break his teeth?
He chewed his nails!

SIX TIMES TABLE

Can you complete the six times table?

Practice question:

$$4 \times 6 = \boxed{24}$$

The Five Minute Test!

1. $1 \times 6 =$

2. $2 \times 6 =$

3. $3 \times 6 =$

4. $4 \times 6 =$

5. $5 \times 6 =$

6. $6 \times 6 =$

7. $7 \times 6 =$

8. $8 \times 6 =$

9. $9 \times 6 =$

10. $10 \times 6 =$

Did you beat the clock?

Check your answers!

Six bars of soap were stolen from a store.
The police say the thieves made a clean getaway!

CREEPY-CRAWLERS

Insects have six legs. How many legs are there altogether in each group of insects?

Practice question:

2 beetles | 12 |

The Five Minute Test!

I. 3 flies

2. 4 ants

3. 6 grasshoppers

4. 5 ladybugs

5. 7 dragonflies

6. 2 bees and I wasp

7. 3 ants and 3 flies

8. 2 butterflies and 2 moths

9. 2 flies and I cricket

10. 5 bees and 4 ladybugs

Did you beat the clock?

Check your answers!

What do bees do with their honey?
They cell it!

SEVEN HEAVEN

Can you complete the seven times table?

Practice question:

$6 \times 7 = \boxed{42}$

The Five Minute Test!

1. $1 \times 7 =$ ☐

2. $2 \times 7 =$ ☐

3. $3 \times 7 =$ ☐

4. $4 \times 7 =$ ☐

5. $5 \times 7 =$ ☐

6. $6 \times 7 =$ ☐

7. $7 \times 7 =$ ☐

8. $8 \times 7 =$ ☐

9. $9 \times 7 =$ ☐

10. $10 \times 7 =$ ☐

Did you beat the clock?

Check your answers!

1. 7 2. 14 3. 21 4. 28 5. 35 6. 42 7. 49 8. 56 9. 63 10. 70

If a long dress is evening wear, what is a suit of armor?
Silverware!

ALL AT SIXES AND SEVENS

The answers to these problems
are below. Can you match the problems
to the answers?

The Five Minute Test!

1. 4 × 7 =

2. 3 × 6 =

3. 6 × 6 =

4. 7 × 7 =

5. 5 × 6 =

6. 6 × 7 =

7. 9 × 7 =

8. 9 × 6 =

9. 10 × 7 =

10. 12 × 6 =

36 72 42 18 30 54
70 49 63 28

Did you beat the clock?

Check your answers!

1. 28 2. 18 3. 36 4. 49 5. 30 6. 42 7. 63 8. 54 9. 70 10. 72

What's the difference between a nail and a boxer?
One's knocked in and the other's knocked out!

STOLEN NUMBERS

Thieves have stolen a number from each problem. Can you replace the numbers?

Practice question:

$\boxed{8} \times 5 = 40$

The Five Minute Test!

1. $6 \times 4 = \boxed{}$

2. $\boxed{} \times 2 = 16$

3. $9 \times \boxed{} = 27$

4. $10 \times 5 = \boxed{}$

5. $\boxed{} \times 6 = 36$

6. $6 \times \boxed{} = 42$

7. $\boxed{} \times 4 = 44$

8. $10 \times 7 = \boxed{}$

9. $7 \times \boxed{} = 49$

10. $\boxed{} \times 5 = 45$

Did you beat the clock?

Check your answers!

What can you hold without ever touching it?
A conversation!

A DATE WITH EIGHT

Can you complete the eight times table?

Practice question:

6 x 8 = $\boxed{48}$

The Five Minute Test!

1. 1 x 8 = ☐

2. 2 x 8 = ☐

3. 3 x 8 = ☐

4. 4 x 8 = ☐

5. 5 x 8 = ☐

6. 6 x 8 = ☐

7. 7 x 8 = ☐

8. 8 x 8 = ☐

9. 9 x 8 = ☐

10. 10 x 8 = ☐

Did you beat the clock?

Check your answers!

What's black and white and has eight wheels?
A penguin on roller skates!

SPROUT ABOUT

The chef cooks eight sprouts per adult and four sprouts per child. How many sprouts does she cook for each table?

Practice question:

2 adults _____16_____ sprouts

The Five Minute Test!

1. 3 adults _____ sprouts

2. 6 adults _____ sprouts

3. 5 adults + 2 children _____ sprouts

4. 4 adults + 1 child _____ sprouts

5. 7 adults _____ sprouts

6. 9 adults _____ sprouts

7. 7 adults + 2 children _____ sprouts

8. 1 adult + 6 children _____ sprouts

9. 11 adults _____ sprouts

10. 10 adults _____ sprouts

Did you beat the clock?

Check your answers!

1. 24 2. 48 3. 48 4. 36 5. 56 6. 72 7. 64 8. 32 9. 88 10. 80

Why are chefs mean?
Because they beat the eggs, mash the potatoes, and whip the cream!

THE WORLD'S WORST TEACHER

Miss Stake has forgotten the times tables.
Can you do them for her?

Practice question:

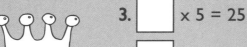

7 x 5 = 35

The Five Minute Test!

1. ☐ x 4 = 32

2. ☐ x 7 = 21

3. ☐ x 5 = 25

4. ☐ x 4 = 40

5. ☐ x 2 = 14

6. ☐ x 7 = 56

7. ☐ x 6 = 48

8. ☐ x 3 = 33

9. ☐ x 7 = 49

10. ☐ x 2 = 18

Did you beat the clock?

Check your answers!

1. 8 2. 3 3. 5 4. 10 5. 7 6. 8 7. 8 8. 11 9. 7 10. 9

What's it called when you throw a rock at a cow and hit a chicken?
A Mis Steak!

TIME FOR NINE

Time to complete the nine times table!

Practice question:

$4 \times 9 =$ 36

The Five Minute Test!

1. $1 \times 9 =$ ☐

2. $2 \times 9 =$ ☐

3. $3 \times 9 =$ ☐

4. $4 \times 9 =$ ☐

5. $5 \times 9 =$ ☐

6. $6 \times 9 =$ ☐

7. $7 \times 9 =$ ☐

8. $8 \times 9 =$ ☐

9. $9 \times 9 =$ ☐

10. $10 \times 9 =$ ☐

Did you beat the clock?

Check your answers!

1. 9 2. 18 3. 27 4. 36 5. 45 6. 54 7. 63 8. 72 9. 81 10. 90

What did the calculator say to his friend?
You can count on me!

TEN DOWN

Complete the ten times table,
starting with the highest numbers.

Practice question:

$2 \times 10 = \boxed{20}$

The Five Minute Test!

1. $12 \times 10 = \boxed{}$

2. $11 \times 10 = \boxed{}$

3. $10 \times 10 = \boxed{}$

4. $9 \times 10 = \boxed{}$

5. $8 \times 10 = \boxed{}$

6. $7 \times 10 = \boxed{}$

7. $6 \times 10 = \boxed{}$

8. $5 \times 10 = \boxed{}$

9. $4 \times 10 = \boxed{}$

10. $3 \times 10 = \boxed{}$

Did you beat the clock?

Check your answers!

Which side of a chicken has the most feathers?
The outside!

SWEET SHOP

Red licorice costs 5¢, black licorice costs 10¢.
How much will these bags of candy cost?

Practice question:

4 black licorice | 40¢ |

The Five Minute Test!

1. 3 red licorice ☐

2. 2 black licorice ☐

3. 6 red licorice ☐

4. 9 black licorice ☐

5. 7 red licorice ☐

6. 11 red licorice ☐

7. 4 red licorice and 2 black licorice ☐

8. 7 red licorice and 5 black licorice ☐

Did you beat the clock?

Check your answers!

1. 15¢ 2. 20¢ 3. 30¢ 4. 90¢ 5. 35¢ 6. 55¢ 7. 40¢ 8. 85¢

What did the teeth say to the steak?
Nice to meat chew!

ELEVEN TIMES TABLE

Can you complete the eleven
times table?

Practice question:

$12 \times 11 = \boxed{132}$

The Five Minute Test!

1. $1 \times 11 = \boxed{}$

2. $2 \times 11 = \boxed{}$

3. $3 \times 11 = \boxed{}$

4. $4 \times 11 = \boxed{}$

5. $5 \times 11 = \boxed{}$

6. $6 \times 11 = \boxed{}$

7. $7 \times 11 = \boxed{}$

8. $8 \times 11 = \boxed{}$

9. $9 \times 11 = \boxed{}$

10. $10 \times 11 = \boxed{}$

Did you beat the clock?

Check your answers!

What happened to the plant in math class?
It grew square roots!

FIND THE SECRET CODE

Complete the problems. Then, write the
answers in order on the code line.

Practice question:

__3__ x 9 = 27

The Five Minute Test!

1. __ × 11 = 22

2. 3 x 3 = __

3. 9 x __ = 36

4. 8 x __ = 64

5. __ × 5 = 35

6. __ × 11 = 44

7. __ × 9 = 72

8. __ × 11 = 99

Code Line: __ __ __ __ __ __ __ __

Did you beat the clock?

Check your answers!

Why don't sharks eat clowns?
Because they taste funny!

TWELVE TIMES TABLE

Whew! The last of the times tables
to complete!

Practice question:

$11 \times 12 =$ 132

The Five Minute Test!

1. $1 \times 12 =$ ☐

2. $2 \times 12 =$ ☐

3. $3 \times 12 =$ ☐

4. $4 \times 12 =$ ☐

5. $5 \times 12 =$ ☐

6. $6 \times 12 =$ ☐

7. $7 \times 12 =$ ☐

8. $8 \times 12 =$ ☐

9. $9 \times 12 =$ ☐

10. $10 \times 12 =$ ☐

Did you beat the clock?

Check your answers!

1. 12 2. 24 3. 36 4. 48 5. 60 6. 72 7. 84 8. 96 9. 108 10. 120

Twelve boxes of perfume have been stolen.
Police dogs are on the scent!

GRUESOME TWOSOME

Use your knowledge of the times tables to solve these problems.

Practice question:

$2 \times 2 = \boxed{4}$

The Five Minute Test!

1. $3 \times 3 =$ ☐

2. $4 \times 4 =$ ☐

3. $5 \times 5 =$ ☐

4. $6 \times 6 =$ ☐

5. $7 \times 7 =$ ☐

6. $8 \times 8 =$ ☐

7. $9 \times 9 =$ ☐

8. $10 \times 10 =$ ☐

9. $11 \times 11 =$ ☐

10. $12 \times 12 =$ ☐

Did you beat the clock?

Check your answers!

Why do birds fly south?
Because it's too far to walk!

BE THE TEACHER

Mark the test by putting a check mark
next to the correct answers and putting an
"X" next to the incorrect ones!

Practice question:

$6 \times 3 = 17$ ☒

The Five Minute Test!

1. $5 \times 4 = 20$ ☐

2. $4 \times 7 = 26$ ☐

3. $6 \times 7 = 42$ ☐

4. $9 \times 4 = 32$ ☐

5. $10 \times 6 = 60$ ☐

6. $5 \times 9 = 48$ ☐

7. $12 \times 3 = 38$ ☐

8. $11 \times 4 = 44$ ☐

9. $12 \times 5 = 70$ ☐

10. $7 \times 9 = 63$ ☐

Did you beat the clock?

Check your answers!

1. ✓ 2. ✗ 3. ✓ 4. ✗ 5. ✓ 6. ✗ 7. ✗ 8. ✓ 9. ✗ 10. ✓

Why did the teacher wear sunglasses?
Because the children were so bright!

THE TIMES-TABLE DETECTIVE

Which times table does each series
of numbers come from?

Practice question:

2 4 6 8 [2] times table

The Five Minute Test!

1. 14 16 18 20 [ ] times table

2. 35 40 45 50 [ ] times table

3. 9 12 15 18 [ ] times table

4. 24 28 32 36 [ ] times table

5. 55 66 77 88 [ ] times table

6. 48 56 64 72 [ ] times table

7. 63 72 81 90 [ ] times table

8. 63 70 77 84 [ ] times table

9. 30 36 42 48 [ ] times table

10. 84 96 108 120 [ ] times table

Did you beat the clock?

Check your answers!

1. 2 2. 5 3. 3 4. 4 5. 11 6. 8 7. 9 8. 7 9. 6 10. 12

Why don't dogs make good dancers?
Because they have two left feet!

BE THE TEACHER AGAIN!

Mark Miss Stake's work with check marks or X's.

Practice question:

11 x 5 = 50 $\boxed{\times}$

The Five Minute Test!

1. 9 x 8 = 72 ☐

2. 12 x 4 = 44 ☐

3. 7 x 6 = 42 ☐

4. 6 x 9 = 56 ☐

5. 10 x 11 = 110 ☐

6. 7 x 8 = 54 ☐

7. 8 x 12 = 94 ☐

8. 7 x 11 = 77 ☐

9. 11 x 12 = 142 ☐

10. 7 x 9 = 64 ☐

Did you beat the clock?

Check your answers!

What do you call a pig that knows karate?
A pork chop!

SUPER SALLY AND LOSING LYNDON

Sally is better at sports than Lyndon.
Figure out how good Sally is by
solving these problems.

The Five Minute Test!

1. Lyndon threw the shot put 4 yards. Sally threw 4 times that. How far did she throw the shotput? _____

2. Lyndon can run 4 laps in 10 minutes. Sally can run 6 times that. How far can she run? _____

3. Lyndon cleared 5 hurdles. Sally cleared 3 times as many. How many hurdles did she clear? _____

4. Lyndon scored 12 runs. Sally scored 10 times as many. How many runs did she score? _____

5. Lyndon scored 6 goals. Sally scored 7 times that number. How many goals did she score?_____

Did you beat the clock?

Check your answers!

1. 16 yards 2. 24 laps 3. 15 hurdles
4. 120 runs 5. 42 goals

Where's the English channel?
I don't know – our television doesn't pick it up!